BUILDINGS AT WORK

Skyscrapers

ELIZABETH ENCARNACION

QED Publishing

QED

First published in the UK in 2007 by
QED Publishing
A Quarto Group company
226 City Road
London EC1V 2TT
www.qed-publishing.co.uk

A catalogue record for this book is available from the British Library.

ISBN 978 1 84538 672 6

Written by Elizabeth Encarnacion
Designed by Rahul Dhiman (Q2A Media)
Series Editor Honor Head
Foldout illustration by Ian Naylor
Picture Researcher Lalit K Dalal/Rituparna Sengupta

Publisher Steve Evans
Creative Director Zeta Davies
Senior Editor Hannah Ray

Printed and bound in China

Picture credits
Key: T = top, B = bottom, C = centre, L = left, R = right, FC = front cover

Words in bold can be found in the Glossary on page 34.

CONTENTS

SKYSCRAPERS

A skyscraper is a very tall building in which people live or work. To people walking on the street below, a skyscraper's top is so high it seems to touch, or scrape, the sky. Different people have different ideas about what makes a building a skyscraper. Some people say that a skyscraper must be at least 150 metres tall. Others think it should just be much taller than the buildings around it. Either way, only the very tallest high-rise buildings are called skyscrapers.

▼ Many big cities are filled with skyscrapers that provide more space to live and work.

The steel revolution

Constructing buildings taller than ten **storeys** was almost impossible until the mid-1800s, when **engineers** discovered how to produce large quantities of **steel** – a material that was far lighter than brick but very strong. Brick buildings with more than a few storeys required the lower floors to have very thick walls to support all the extra weight of the floors above. Steel meant that the walls could be the same thickness throughout the whole building, making it easier to build higher.

▲ Tall skyscrapers would not be possible without strong steel beams.

▼ The Chrysler Building's roof has lights that make it shine at night.

MAKE IT PRETTY

Architects **often add decorative touches when they are designing** skyscrapers. The Chrysler Building in New York City was built in the 1920s as the headquarters for the Chrysler car company. The architect decided to change his plans to make some of the decoration on the building look like parts of a car. The spire **and roof were covered with shiny** stainless steel**, and large copies of** hood ornaments **and** radiator caps **were used as decorations and** gargoyles.

EARLY SKYSCRAPERS

In the early 1900s, builders in New York, in the United States, were racing to be the first to construct the tallest skyscrapers in the world. The race to build the tallest building became so competitive that the architect of the Chrysler Building announced a false height for the building. Soon after, the Manhattan Company skyscraper was declared the tallest building in the world. Then, in 1930, the architect installed the spire on top of the Chrysler Building and stole the title. The next year, the Empire State Building was finished at a height of 443 metres and remained the world's tallest building for 41 years.

Many early skyscrapers, such ➤ as the Empire State Building, are still used today.

The first skyscraper

Compared with modern skyscrapers, the first high-rise buildings seem tiny. However, early skyscrapers like the Home Insurance Building in Chicago, USA, were the first to use steel columns and **beams** to make the structures lighter so they could be thinner and taller. This **technology** is still used today to make skyscrapers reach the sky.

The Home Insurance Building ➤ was built in 1885. It was only twelve storeys tall but it was the first skyscraper.

BEFORE SKYSCRAPERS

When it was completed in 1873, the Midland Grand Hotel (now known as St Pancras Chambers) in London was the largest hotel in the world. It used many of the new ideas that helped make the first skyscrapers possible. Concrete was used to make the floors strong and fireproof. Hydraulic ascending rooms, **an early type of lift, were installed to help hotel guests to reach their rooms more easily.**

◀ The clock tower on St Pancras Chambers is 82 metres tall.

THE WORLD'S TALLEST

Most experts consider Taipei 101, built in 2004, to be the world's tallest building.

In 1998, the Petronas Towers in Kuala Lumpur, Malaysia, claimed the title of the world's tallest building because its spires were taller than the roof of the Sears Tower in Chicago. However, the Sears Tower had **antennae** that were even taller than the Petronas Towers' spires, so it claimed it was still the tallest. To solve the argument, an international group of engineers created four categories of tallest buildings. The first category is for the building that is tallest from the ground floor to the top of the spire. The second is for the building with the highest floor where people live or work. The third category is for the building that is the tallest from its ground floor to its roof, and the fourth is for the building that is tallest from the ground floor to the top of the antenna. Taiwan's Taipei 101 is now at the top in the first three categories, but the Sears Tower still has the tallest antenna.

ANTENNA ANTICS

With its tallest antenna reaching 86.3 metres above its roof, the Sears Tower is now the tallest skyscraper measured from its base to the top of its antenna. The Sears Tower actually has two antennae – the shorter one measures 77 metres. The two antennae are lit up in different colours at different times of the year. In March, the antennae are lit green for St Patrick's Day. In October, they are orange for Halloween, and in December they are red and green for the holiday season.

▲ Aeroplane warning lights at the top of the Sears Tower's two antennae flash 40 times a minute.

Going up

Double-decker lifts in Taipei 101 can carry twice as many people to higher floors without taking up more room in the **vertical core**. These are express lifts that take workers directly to a **sky lobby** on a much higher floor where they can change to another lift to reach the floors above that point. The lobbies are also double-decker, and usually have escalators running between the paired floors.

▲ Double-decker lifts are two lifts, one on top of the other. This means that two floors can use the lift at the same time.

FACT!

Taipei 101's double-decker express lifts can travel at 63 kilometres per hour!

SUPERSKYSCRAPERS

Just as New York architects raced to construct the tallest skyscrapers in the early 1900s, today's skyscrapers are being built higher and higher to break the record. Having the world's tallest building can give a city, or even an entire country, a strong sense of pride, and attract tourists to visit in greater numbers. In fact, there are many superskyscrapers currently being built or planned that could become the world's tallest in one or more category. The Freedom Tower, being built at the site of the World Trade Center in New York City, was designed with an antenna that will reach 541.3 metres. That's 1776 feet, which symbolizes the year America declared its independence.

This computer drawing shows ➤ what the New York City skyline might look like once the Freedom Tower is built.

FACT!

It will take three to four months to clean all the windows of the completed Burj Dubai.

BURJ DUBAI

Just as the architect of the Chrysler Building kept its real height a secret so that his skyscraper would be the tallest, no one really knows how tall the Burj Dubai will be when it is finished. Now under construction in the United Arab Emirates, Burj Dubai is expected to become the new all-round record holder at over 700 metres high, with more than 120 floors.

◄ This drawing shows what the Burj Dubai building will look like when it is completed.

Shanghai World Financial Centre

Some people thought the Shanghai World Financial Centre in China would be the tallest building in the world when it was completed, but a plan has been announced for the skyscraper to **top out** at only 492 metres, slightly shorter than Taipei 101. Of course, the plan could still change. A large, circular hole in the top floors of the building has already been redesigned as a rectangle that builders say will be easier to construct.

▲ The hole in the top of the Shanghai World Financial Centre reduces the force of the wind pushing against the building and gives it a unique look.

TWIN TOWERS

Sometimes it is easier to build two skyscrapers instead of one huge building that could hold the same number of people. As buildings become taller, the **central core** that contains the lifts, emergency stairs and other services takes up a greater area. That means less room is available on each floor for work or living space. Offices in a building that is wider and deeper are more likely to be without windows. However, with twin skyscrapers such as the Petronas Towers in Kuala Lumpur, more workers can fit in a small area with lots of natural light.

The Petronas Towers ➤ are the tallest twin towers in the world.

FACT!

The Petronas Towers are connected by a two-level bridge at the 41st and 42nd floors that allows people to cross from one building into the other. It has expansion joints that allow the towers to move slightly without damaging the bridge.

Leaning towers

Most leaning towers lean because they're starting to fall down. However, the twin towers of the Puerta de Europa in Madrid, Spain, were made to lean towards each other. The architect wanted to design two buildings that would form a gateway. ('Puerta' means gateway in Spanish.) These twin towers are so similar that their **helipads** had to be painted different colours so helicopter pilots could tell them apart from the air!

▲ Each of these towers leans three times as much as the Leaning Tower of Pisa in Italy.

NEW YORK'S TWIN TOWERS

The World Trade Center in New York City was actually a complex of seven high-rise buildings, with the super-tall twin towers as the centrepiece. These famous buildings, which were the tallest in the world when they were completed in 1973, still influence the way skyscrapers are designed, even though they are no longer standing. For example, express lifts with sky lobbies, similar to the ones in Taipei 101, were first used in the Twin Towers.

◀ The Twin Towers of the World Trade Center solved many problems that had kept skyscrapers from reaching greater heights.

STEEL FRAMES

A steel frame acts like a person's skeleton, supporting the building and keeping everything in its place. Steel is one of the strongest building materials, but it is light enough to use in very tall buildings without having to add any extra support on the lower floors. However, steel is more expensive than some other construction materials, and it can be damaged by rust or the heat from a fire.

Large cranes are used ➤ to lift the heavy steel beams into place.

14

FACT!
The city of Hong Kong has nearly 8000 skyscrapers.

Curtain wall
an outer wall that does not support the building

81

Tuned mass damper
computers move a heavy weight from side to side to keep the skyscraper from swaying in strong winds

ventilation systems
provide clean air and move it around the building

Antenna
the height helps transmit radio or television waves further without other buildings to block them

Structural top
the highest part of the building that cannot be removed

Sky high

Skyscraper construction workers can't be afraid of heights, but they are careful about safety! Harnesses attached to safety lines keep them from falling off the building, and helmets protect their heads from anything falling from above. Special temporary lifts on the side of the building carry them up to the top of the building and back down again.

▶ Builders use this lift on the outside of a skyscraper that is under construction.

Lift shafts
lifts travel up and down inside hollow lift shafts

Concrete core
the strong 'backbone'. Helps keep the building stable

Emergency stairs
used when fire or power cuts make the lifts unsafe

Sky lobby
intermediate floors where people can change from an express lift to another lift or staircase

Hot stuff

After a crane lifts them into place, steel beams are bolted or welded together to create a strong, permanent connection. Then, the beams are sprayed with a **fireproof coating** so they will not weaken if a fire starts inside the building.

► **Welders** must wear protective gear such as welding helmets, goggles, and heavy gloves.

CURTAINS

If the steel frame is a skeleton, then the curtain wall is the skin of the skyscraper. A curtain wall does not help to support the weight of the building like a brick wall on a house does. Instead, it covers the building, shielding the people inside the building from natural elements like rain, heat and wind. Curtain walls can also be decorative, as on the Empire State Building where they give the building its classic, limestone-covered appearance, or on a glass-covered skyscraper with a sleek, modern look.

► The smooth, glass walls of many skyscrapers are supported by steel frames.

REINFORCED CONCRETE

Concrete is made from water, cement and gravel or sand. Concrete is very strong against forces that squeeze it together (such as gravity pulling down on it), but not as strong when forces bend it (such as wind pushing on a skyscraper). To make it stronger against these forces, builders reinforce the concrete by pouring it over a grid of small steel rods and letting it dry. Reinforced concrete is very cheap to produce. The concrete can take a long time to dry, which slows down construction, but new, fast-drying concretes are being developed to solve that problem.

◄ Concrete poured around steel rods is a cheaper building method than using steel frames.

Crazy cranes

Construction crews use giant cranes to lift building materials up to the top of the skyscraper. Sometimes the cranes are designed to climb up the building as it gets taller and taller. The cranes used on skyscrapers are often so huge that they're too big to transport to the building site in one piece, so they're put together onsite by smaller cranes.

19

► Large skyscrapers often need more than one crane to lift all the building materials.

Bedrock
the hard rock underneath the soil. Foundations are dug into the bedrock.

Spread footing
pyramid shape spreads the building's weight over a wider surface

Steel frame
the inner 'skeleton' of a skyscraper that gives it its shape

Office floor
may be open-plan, like this, or separated into smaller rooms

CROSS-BRACING

Wind pushes against skyscrapers with great force, and can make them sway back and forth. The people working or living inside might feel uncomfortable, or even sick, if the building was moving all the time. Adding diagonal braces to the outside of the skyscraper can help strengthen the structure against the wind. IM Pei, a famous architect, designed the Bank of China Tower in Hong Kong so that the cross-bracing would be part of the outer wall and the skyscraper thought of as a working piece of art.

◄ The triangles on the outer walls of this building give it strength against natural forces.

A good foundation

Foundations act like the feet of the skyscraper. They support the weight of everything above them and spread that weight out across the ground below. First, columns made from steel or reinforced concrete are placed into holes in the ground or deep soil. Then, the builders insert steel **reinforcing rods** and pour concrete around the rods and the columns to make strong foundations. The steel or reinforced concrete frame of the building is then connected to the foundations.

▼ Diggers dig out holes in the **bedrock** for the foundations of a skyscraper.

THE BACKBONE

Many modern skyscrapers are built with a hollow concrete core surrounded by steel framing. This method produces a lighter, more open, steel-frame construction while at the same time giving the building a strong backbone that can help keep it steady. The concrete core contains the lift shafts, emergency stairs, air ducts and other central services.

► Some skyscrapers are engineered to have both reinforced concrete and steel beams.

FACT!
The CITIC Plaza in Guangzhou, China, is the tallest concrete building in the world at 391 metres.

RADICAL RAFT

Architects planning the Broadgate Tower in London faced a unique problem: the skyscraper was to be built on a concrete and steel raft over a railway tunnel. This meant that the foundation could not support the weight of a concrete core. Instead, the architects designed a cross-braced outer wall that would support the structure, while spreading out the forces of gravity and wind.

The Broadgate Tower was ➤ designed with cross-bracing that makes it light but strong.

▼ Each X-shape on the outer walls of the John Hancock Center is between sixteen and eighteen storeys tall.

X marks the spot

Chicago, USA, is often called the Windy City. High-rise builders had to come up with ways of protecting their buildings from the strong winds that are common in the city. Cross-bracing was used to prevent the John Hancock Center from being moved about by the powerful wind. The giant X-shapes on the outside of the building mean fewer support beams were needed on the inside. More of the interior of the building could therefore be used for work and living spaces without large columns getting in the way.

FIGHTING NATURE

Some skyscrapers are built in places where earthquakes and hurricanes are common. Powerful, sudden forces pushing against the sides of a building could damage it, so architects study the effects of these natural forces and find ways of keeping the structure steady. The Jin Mao Tower in Shanghai, China, has a strong concrete core that acts like a backbone, keeping it stiff even in a strong earthquake or the 200 km/h winds of a major typhoon.

◀ At 421 metres tall, the Jin Mao Tower has many systems to stop it swaying in the wind.

Earthquake-proof

Mexico City is right in the centre of one of the world's most active earthquake zones. Designers had to use the most up-to-date technology to fight the forces of earthquakes while building the Torre Mayor, the tallest building in Latin America. One system uses 98 giant **shock absorbers** to reduce the movement of the building and its parts.

WILD WIND

Some skyscrapers, such as the Citicorp Center in New York and Taipei 101 in Taiwan, use a tuned mass damper to reduce movement caused by wind. Taipei 101's damper is a 660 tonne ball. When the building leans one way, the ball slowly starts to follow, but by that time the building is already trying to lean back the other way. The mass of the ball is so great that it pulls the building back towards the centre, reducing the movement.

Some skyscrapers have a large weight in their upper floors to slow down the building's movement. ▶

FACT!

The swimming pool on the 57th floor of the Jin Mao Tower acts as a damper to reduce the building's movement in strong winds!

◀ 1700 construction workers helped to build the Torre Mayor in Mexico City.

25

EXTREME TEMPERATURES

When planning a new skyscraper, an architect must think about the weather in that location. Very hot or very cold temperatures may create problems that the architect must remember in his or her design. The Burj Al Arab, which is located on a man-made island just off the coast of Dubai, is the tallest hotel building in the world at 321 metres. Its windows face the cooler water out at sea, while a special **fibreglass fabric** on the side facing the desert coast helps repel heat and provide soft, filtered light inside.

◄ The Burj Al Arab's shape was inspired by an Arabian sailing ship.

LET IT SNOW

One Liberty Place in Philadelphia, USA, has a tiered, sloping roof that could become dangerous for the people walking below if snow or ice collected on it. As a result, this skyscraper was designed with a system that melts the ice and snow off the outside walls before it can become a problem.

Skyscrapers in cold areas must ▶ protect people on the pavement below from falling snow and ice.

FACT!

The Al Faisaliah Center in the desert city of Riyadh, Saudi Arabia, freezes as many as 50 000 kilograms of ice each night. The building's cooling system lets the ice melt during the day to help chill the air.

◀ Outer walls without windows can help keep a building cooler.

Hot, hot, hot

In the hot desert climate of Jeddah, Saudi Arabia, an outer wall of windows would make it very difficult to keep the building cool. The National Commerce Bank was designed with most of the windows facing in towards a central **atrium**. Three large holes in the building's outer wall allow indirect sunlight to filter into the offices, providing natural light without too much heat. Gardens growing in the open areas created by the large holes mean office workers have an attractive, green view.

GREEN SKYSCRAPERS

Today's builders are working hard to make their skyscrapers 'green'. These buildings are not painted green, but are designed to save energy and use fewer **natural resources**. Some even bring the outdoors inside. The Commerzbank Tower in Frankfurt, Germany, has nine 'sky gardens' spread throughout the building. Each office in the skyscraper has a view of either the city or an indoor garden. Natural light hits every office window, which means that workers do not need to use so many artificial lights and therefore use less electricity. The open areas inside the building create natural airflow, reducing the costs of **air conditioning**.

Many buildings, like the Commerzbank Tower, (right) use natural light, ventilation shafts, and indoor gardens to save energy. ➤

The Gherkin

30 St Mary Axe is also known as 'the Gherkin' because of its unusual shape. Many of the building materials used in the structure were either recycled, or designed to be reused in the future. The building's design also helps to save energy by reducing the need for artificial light, heating and air conditioning. For example, the Gherkin's distinctive **tinted** glass reduces the amount of heat absorbed by the building, making it cooler.

The Gherkin uses ➤ only half the energy a traditional skyscraper of its size would use.

FULL OF ENERGY

The Condé Nast Building at 4 Times Square is famous for being the first environmentally friendly skyscraper in New York. Fuel cells **and** solar panels in the building help reduce the amount of electricity needed from outside sources. A state-of-the-art system filters the air, making it a healthier environment in which to work. Recycling chutes deliver reusable waste to storage areas, where it is picked up and taken to recycling centres.

◀ The curtain wall of the Condé Nast Building shades and **insulates** the offices inside so less heat or air conditioning is needed.

SPECIAL SKYSCRAPERS

Architects have to keep many things in mind while they are designing new skyscrapers. City **building codes**, strong natural forces and what the building will be used for are all important factors to consider. But the architect also wants the building to look good and attract attention. The HSB Turning Torso building in Sweden looks like a giant work of art because the architect copied the shape of a sculpture that he had created in the past. When it was built, it was the only 'twisting' skyscraper, but it has already inspired new skyscraper designs in other countries.

The Turning Torso skyscraper is ➤ made up of nine cubes that appear to twist around the central core.

FACT!

Cranes could not be used during construction of the Turning Torso because of its curving design. Instead, the building's lifts were installed in stages to haul the building materials up to the higher floors.

BUILDING BLOCKS

The Nakagin Capsule Tower in Tokyo, Japan, was built with 140 individual apartments, or capsules, all stacked in different directions and attached to a central concrete core. Each capsule has its own furniture and appliances built into the walls. Televisions, radios and even calculators have also been installed. The units were designed so they could be easily taken apart to be modernized or replaced.

◄ Each apartment in the Nakagin Capsule Tower was constructed at a factory before being lifted into place by a large crane and bolted to the concrete core.

Around the globe

A large, golden sphere sits just below the spire of the Al Faisaliah Center in Riyadh, Saudi Arabia. This tinted glass-covered bubble has a multi-level restaurant inside, allowing diners to enjoy amazing views of the city in every direction.

➤ The Al Faisaliah Center may have been designed to remind people of a ballpoint pen.

TALL TOWERS

Skyscrapers are not the tallest structures in the world. In fact, many towers like the CN Tower in Toronto, Canada, reach higher into the sky than the tallest skyscrapers. The CN Tower is the world's tallest freestanding structure on land, but it is not considered a skyscraper because it is not a place for people to live or work around the clock. Some **communications** towers, often called masts, are built even taller, so that radio and television signals can reach more homes. They are supported by wires that stop them from falling down.

At 553.3 metres tall, the ► CN Tower is taller than the world's tallest skyscraper.

▲ The tall Glasgow Tower has a motor that can rotate it into the wind.

Going round in circles

The Glasgow Tower at the Glasgow Science Centre in Scotland is the only building in the world that can turn in circles. The tower is shaped like an aeroplane's wing, which reduces the force of the wind on the structure. To work properly, the wing shape must face into the wind, so the tower's base has a motor that can turn it in any direction.

GLOSSARY

air conditioning A system that spreads cooled air throughout a building.

air ducts Hollow metal tubes through which air flows from one place to another, often used in heating and air conditioning systems.

antennae Metal rods that send or receive radio waves.

architects People who design buildings and oversee their construction.

atrium An open area inside a building which extends upwards for several storeys.

beams Strong pieces of metal or wood used as a support in a building.

bedrock The solid layer of rock beneath the soil or sand on the Earth's surface.

building codes Rules and laws that builders follow during construction to make buildings safe.

capsules A living-unit that is made in a factory then transported to the building site to be installed.

central core A strong column in the centre of a skyscraper that surrounds the lifts and stairways and supports the building. Also called the vertical core.

central services The basic service and supply systems of a building, such as lifts, stairways, rubbish chutes, and lobbies.

communications A system for passing information from one place to another, such as telephones.

complex A group of buildings connected by passageways or underground tunnels.

concrete A very strong building material made by mixing water and cement with gravel or sand.

cross-bracing Diagonal beams used to support the structure of a building and reduce movement.

curtain wall An outside wall that does not help support the weight of a building.

engineers People who design machines or other technology.

fibreglass fabric A very strong fabric made from fine glass fibres.

fireproof coating A material that covers steel beams and makes them more difficult to damage with fire.

frame The structure underneath the outer surface of a building that gives it strength.

fuel cells Devices that change chemical energy into electricity without much waste or pollution.

gargoyles Sculptures, often in the shape of a strange-looking human or animal, designed to drain rainwater away from a building.

helipad A hard surface on which helicopters can take off and land.

hood ornaments Metallic decorations on the front of a car, often shaped like an animal.

hydraulic ascending rooms Early types of lift moved by pressurized liquid.

insulates Protects from the weather and extreme temperatures.

lift shafts Hollow passages inside a building in which a lift travels up and down.

limestone A rock, often used in building, that is mostly made up of shells and the skeletons of marine life.

natural resources   Useful materials that are found in nature, such as trees and fresh water.

radiator caps   Round, metallic lids that close the container of water which cools the engine of a car.

raft   A type of foundation, with supports like a bridge, that allows architects to construct buildings on soft soil or uneven land.

reinforcing rods   Used to give a building strength and support.

shock absorbers   Devices that absorb sudden bursts of energy, such as earthquake tremors, to reduce the up-and-down movement of a building.

sky lobbies   Public floors halfway up a high-rise building where people can change from one set of lifts to another.

solar panels   Flat sheets of glass that turn solar energy into electricity.

spire   A pointed roof or thin projection on the top of a building.

stainless steel   A combination of two metals that does not rust easily.

steel   A strong metal building material.

storeys   Levels or floors of a building.

technology   The study of how to solve everyday problems with tools.

tiered   A roof with layers that slope upwards in a step-like pattern.

tinted   Partially shaded, like sunglasses.

top out   To reach the highest point of construction on a skyscraper.

tuned mass damper   A device that absorbs energy from strong forces to reduce the side-to-side movement of a building.

vertical core   A strong column in the centre of a skyscraper that surrounds the lifts and stairways and supports the building.

welded   When metal pieces are joined together using extreme heat to melt them and then pushing them together until the metal cools and hardens.

welder   A construction worker who uses heat to join pieces of metal together.

Websites

Learn more about the forces that push against a skyscraper:
http://www.pbs.org/wgbh/buildingbig/skyscraper/index.html

Watch an animation of Taipei 101's tuned mass damper at work:
http://www.motioneering.ca/Public/Taipei101Animation.aspx

Get more information about specific buildings
http://www.emporis.com
Click on buildings in the blue bar.

Take a virtual skyscraper tour of New York City
http://www.skyscraper.org/webwalk/map4.html

INDEX